MW01124276

ISBN: 9781290620345

Published by:
HardPress Publishing
8345 NW 66TH ST #2561
MIAMI FL 33166-2626

Email: info@hardpress.net
Web: http://www.hardpress.net

A

Discourse,

DELIVERED AT PLYMOUTH,

DECEMBER 22, 1820.

In Commemoration of

THE FIRST

SETTLEMENT OF NEW-ENGLAND.

BY

DANIEL WEBSTER.

BOSTON:

WELLS AND LILLY,——COURT-STREET.

1821.

F
68
W37

DISTRICT OF MASSACHUSETTS, TO WIT:

District Clerk's Office.

BE it remembered, that on the twentieth day of December, A. D. 1821, in the forty-sixth year of the Independence of the United States of America, Wells & Lilly of the said District, have deposited in this Office the title of a Book, the Right whereof they claim as Proprietors, in the Words following, *to wit* :—

" A Discourse, delivered at Plymouth, December 22, 1820. In commemoration of the First Settlement of New-England. By Daniel Webster."

In Conformity to the Act of the Congress of the United States, entitled, " An Act for the Encouragement of Learning, by securing the copies of Maps, Charts, and Books, to the Authors and Proprietors of such Copies, during the times therein mentioned :" and also to an Act entitled, " An Act supplementary to an Act, entitled, An Act for the Encouragement of Learning, by securing the Copies of Maps, Charts, and Books, to the Authors and Proprietors of such Copies during the times therein mentioned : and extending the benefits thereof to the Arts of Designing, Engraving, and Etching Historical and other Prints."

JNO. W. DAVIS,
Clerk of the District of Massachusetts.

PLYMOUTH, *Dec.* 23, 1820.

HON. DANIEL WEBSTER,

SIR,

AT a meeting of the Trustees of the PILGRIM SOCIETY, present, *John Watson, William Davis, James Sever, Alden Bradford, Barnabas Hedge, Thomas Jackson, Jr.* and *Zabdiel Sampson,* Esquires, VOTED, " That the thanks of the Trustees be presented to the HON. DANIEL WEBSTER, for his eloquent and interesting DISCOURSE, delivered at Plymouth, on the 22d instant, at their request, in commemoration of the completion of the second century since the settlement of *New England*—that he be requested to furnish a copy for publication—and that the Corresponding Secretary communicate the preceding vote."

While in the performance of this duty, as honorable as it is pleasing, I am directed to subjoin, that the Committee of the *Massachusetts Historical Society,* and of the *American Antiquarian Society,* who attended on this occasion, by invitation, unite in the request.

With great esteem and regard,

I am, Sir,

Very Respectfully,

SAMUEL DAVIS,
Corresponding Secretary of the Pilgrim Society.

BOSTON, *Dec.* 26, 1820.

SIR,

I HAVE received yours of the 23d, communicating the request of the Trustees of the Pilgrim Society, and of the Committee of the Historical and Antiquarian Societies, that a copy of my Discourse may be furnished for the press. I shall cheerfully comply with this request; but at the same time I must add, that such is the nature of my other engagements, that I hope I may be pardoned if I should be compelled to postpone this compliance to a more distant day than I could otherwise have wished.

I am, Sir, with true regard,

Your most obedient Servant,

DANIEL WEBSTER.

To SAMUEL DAVIS, *Esq.*
Corresponding Secretary of the Pilgrim Society.

DISCOURSE.

LET us rejoice that we behold this day. Let us be thankful that we have lived to see the bright and happy breaking of the auspicious morn, which commences the third century of the history of New-England. Auspicious indeed; bringing a happiness beyond the common allotment of Providence to men; full of present joy, and gilding with bright beams the prospect of futurity, is the dawn that awakens us to the commemoration of the Landing of the Pilgrims.

Living at an epoch which naturally marks the progress of the history of our native land, we have come hither to celebrate the great event

2

with which that history commenced. Forever
honoured be this, the place of our father's refuge! Forever remembered the day which saw
them, weary and distressed, broken in every
thing but spirit, poor in all but faith and courage, at last secure from the dangers of wintry
seas, and impressing this shore with the first
footsteps of civilized man!

It is a noble faculty of our nature which ena-
bles us to connect our thoughts, our sympathies,
and our happiness, with what is distant, in place
or time; and, looking before and after, to hold
communion at once with our ancestors and our
posterity. Human and mortal although we are,
we are nevertheless not mere insulated beings,
without relation to the past or the future. Neither the point of time, nor the spot of earth, in
which we physically live, bounds our rational
and intellectual enjoyments. We live in the
past by a knowledge of its history; and in the
future by hope and anticipation. By ascend-
ing to an association with our ancestors; by contemplating their example and studying their

character; by partaking their sentiments, and imbibing their spirit; by accompanying them in their toils, by sympathising in their sufferings, and rejoicing in their successes and their triumphs, we mingle our own existence with theirs, and seem to belong to their age. We become their contemporaries, live the lives which they lived, endure what they endured, and partake in the rewards which they enjoyed.. And in like manner, by running along the line of future time, by contemplating the probable fortunes of those who are coming after us; by attempting something which may promote their happiness, and leave some not dishonourable memorial of ourselves for their regard, when we shall sleep with the fathers, we protract our own earthly being, and seem to crowd whatever is future, as well as all that is past, into the narrow compass of our earthly existence. As it is not a vain and false, but an exalted and religious imagination, which leads us to raise our thoughts from the orb, which, amidst this universe of worlds, the Creator has given us to inhabit, and to send them with something of the feeling which nature prompts, and teaches to be proper among children of the same Eternal Parent, to the contemplation of the myriads of fellow beings, with which his goodness has peopled the infinite of space ;—so neither is it false or vain to consider ourselves as interested and connected with our whole race, through all time ; allied to our ancestors ; allied to our posterity ; closely compacted on all sides with others; ourselves being but links in the great chain of being, which begins with the origin of our race, runs onward through its successive generations, binding together the past, the present, and the future, and terminating at last, with the consummation of all things earthly, at the throne of God.

There may be, and there often is, indeed, a regard for ancestry, which nourishes only a weak pride ; as there is also a care for posterity, which only disguises an habitual avarice, or hides the workings of a low and groveling vanity. But there is also a moral and philosophical respect for our ancestors, which elevates the character and improves the heart. Next to the sense of. religious duty and moral feeling, I hardly know what should bear with stronger obligation on a liberal and enlightened mind, than a consciousness of alliance with excellence which is departed; and a consciousness, too, that in its acts and conduct, and even in its sentiments and thoughts, it may be actively operating on the happiness of those who come after it. Poetry is found to have few stronger conceptions, by which it would affect or overwhelm the mind, than those in which it presents the moving and speaking image of the departed dead to the senses of the living. This belongs to poetry, only because it is congenial to our nature. Poetry is, in this respect, but the hand-maid of true philosophy and morality; it deals with us as human beings, naturally reverencing those whose visible connexion with this state of existence is severed, and who may yet exercise we know not what sympathy with ourselves;——and when it carries us forward, also, and shows us the long continued result of all the good we do, in the prosperity of those who follow us, till it bears us from ourselves, and absorbs us in an intense interest for what shall happen to the generations after us, it speaks only in the language of our nature, and affects us with sentiments which belong to us as human beings.

Standing in this relation to our ancestors and our posterity, we are assembled on this memorable spot, to perform the duties which that relation, and the present occasion, impose upon us. We have come to this Rock, to record here our homage for our Pilgrim Fathers; our sympathy in their sufferings; our gratitude for their labours; our admiration of their virtues; our veneration for their piety; and our attachment to those principles of civil and religious liberty, which they encountered the dangers of the ocean, the storms of heaven, the violence of savages, disease, exile, and famine, to enjoy and to establish.——And we would leave here, also, for the generations which are rising up rapidly to fill our places, some proof, that we have endeavoured to transmit the great inheritance unimpaired; that in our estimate of public principles, and private virtue; in our veneration of religion and piety; in our devotion to civil and religious liberty; in our regard to whatever advances human knowledge, or improves human happiness, we are not altogether unworthy of our origin.

There is a local feeling, connected with this occasion, too strong to be resisted; a sort of *genius of the place*, which inspires and awes us. We feel that we are on the spot, where the first scene of our history was laid; where the hearths and altars of New-England were first placed; where Christianity, and civilization, and letters made their first lodgment, in a vast extent of country, covered with a wilderness, and peopled by roving barbarians. We are here, at the season of the year at which the event took place. The imagination irresistibly and rapidly draws around us the principal features, and the leading characters in the original scene. We cast our eyes abroad on the ocean, and we see where the little barque, with the interesting group upon its deck, made its slow progress to the shore. We look around us, and behold the hills and promontories, where the anxious eyes of our fathers first saw the places of habitation and of rest. We feel the cold which benumbed, and listen to the winds which pierced them. Beneath us is the Rock, on which New-England received the feet of the Pilgrims. We seem even to behold them, as they struggle with the elements, and, with toilsome efforts gain the shore. We listen to the chiefs in council ; we see the unexampled exhibition of female fortitude and resignation ; we hear the whisperings of youthful impatience, and we see, what a painter of our own has also represented by his pencil, chilled and shivering childhood, houseless, but for a mother's arms, couchless, but for a mother's breast, till our own blood almost freezes. The mild dignity of CARVER and of BRADFORD; the decisive and soldier-like air and manner of STANDISH ; the devout BREW-STER; the enterprising ALLERTON; the general firmness and thoughtfulness of the whole band; their conscious joy for dangers escaped ; their deep solicitude about dangers to come; their trust in heaven; their high religious faith, full of confidence and anticipation :—all these seem to belong to this place, and to be present upon this occasion, to fill us with reverence and admiration.

The settlement of New-England by the colony
which landed here on the twenty second of December, sixteen hundred and twenty, although
not the first European establishment in what
now constitutes the United States, was yet so
peculiar in its causes and character, and has
been followed, and must still be followed, by
such consequences, as to give it a high claim
to lasting commemoration. On these causes
and consequences, more than on its immediately attendant circumstances, its importance
as an historical event depends. Great actions
and striking occurrences, having excited a temporary admiration, often pass away and are forgotten, because they leave no lasting results, af-
fecting the prosperity and happiness of communities. Such is frequently the fortune of the
most brilliant military achievements. Of the ten
thousand battles which have been fought; of
all the fields fertilized with carnage; of the
banners which have been bathed in blood; of
the warriors who have hoped that they had risen
from the field of conquest to a glory as bright
and as durable as the stars, how few that con-

tinue long to interest mankind! The victory of
yesterday is reversed by the defeat of to-day;
the star of military glory, rising like a meteor,
like a meteor has fallen; disgrace and disaster
hang on the heels of conquest and renown; vic-
tor and vanquished presently pass away to oblivion,
and the world goes on in its course, with the
loss only of so many lives and so much treasure.

But if this be frequently, or generally, the fortune of military achievements, it is not always so.
There are enterprises, military as well as civil,
which sometimes check the current of events,
give a new turn to human affairs, and transmit
their consequences through ages. We see their
importance in their results, and call them great,
because great things follow. There have been
battles which have fixed the fate of nations.
These come down to us in history with a solid
and permanent interest, not created by a display
of glittering armour, the rush of adverse bat-
talions, the sinking and rising of pennons, the
flight, the pursuit, and the victory; but by their
effect in advancing or retarding human knowledge,
in overthrowing or establishing despotism, in ex-

tending or destroying human happiness. When the traveller pauses on the plain of Marathon, what are the emotions which most strongly agitate his breast? What is that glorious recollection, which thrills through his frame, and suffuses his eyes?—Not, I imagine, that Grecian skill and Grecian valour were here most signally displayed; but that Greece herself was here saved. It is, because to this spot, and to the event which has rendered it immortal, he refers all the succeeding glories of the republic. It is because if that day had gone otherwise, Greece had perished. It is because he perceives that her philosophers, and orators, her poets and painters, her sculptors and architects, her governments and free institutions, point backward to Marathon, and that their future existence seems to have been suspended on the contingency, whether the Persian or the Grecian banner should wave victorious in the beams of that day's setting sun. And as his imagination kindles at the retrospect, he is transported back to the interesting moment, he counts the fearful odds of the contending hosts, his interest for the result overwhelms him; he

trembles, as if it were still uncertain, and seems
to doubt, whether he may consider Socrates and
Plato, Demosthenes, Sophocles and Phidias, as
secure, yet, to himself and to the world.

" If we conquer," said the Athenian commander
on the morning of that decisive day,—" If we
conquer, we shall make Athens the greatest city
of Greece." A prophecy, how well fulfilled !—
" If God prosper us," might have been the more
appropriate language of our Fathers, when they
landed upon this Rock ;—" if God prosper us,
we shall here begin a work which shall last for
ages ; we shall plant here a new society, in the
principles of the fullest liberty, and the purest
religion : we shall subdue this wilderness which
is before us ; we shall fill this region of the great
continent, which stretches almost from pole to
pole, with civilization and christianity ; the
temples of the true God shall rise, where now
ascends the smoke of idolatrous sacrifice ; fields
and gardens, the flowers of summer, and the wav-
ing and golden harvests of autumn, shall extend
over a thousand hills, and stretch along a thousand

vallies, never yet, since the creation, reclaimed to the use of civilized man. We shall whiten this coast with the canvass of a prosperous commerce ; we shall stud the long and winding shore with an hundred cities. That which we sow in weakness shall be raised in strength. From our sincere but houseless worship, there shall spring splendid temples to record God's goodness ; from the simplicity of our social union, there shall arise wise and politic constitutions of government, full of the liberty which we ourselves bring and breathe ; from our zeal for learning, institutions shall spring, which shall scatter the light of knowledge throughout the land, and, in time, paying back where they have borrowed, shall contribute their part to the great aggregate of human knowledge ; and our descendants, through all generations, shall look back to this spot, and to this hour, with unabated affection and regard."

A brief remembrance of the causes which led to the settlement of this place ; some account of the peculiarities and characteristic qualities of that settlement, as distinguished from other instances of colonization; a short notice of the progress of New-England in the great interests of Society, during the century which is now elapsed; with a few observations on the principles upon which society and government are established in this country;—comprise all that can be attempted, and much more than can be satisfactorily performed on the present occasion.

Of the motives which influenced the first settlers to a voluntary exile, induced them to relinquish their native country, and to seek an asylum in this then unexplored wilderness, the first and principal, no doubt, were connected with Religion. They sought to enjoy a higher degree of Religious freedom, and what they esteemed a purer form of Religious worship, than was allowed to their choice, or presented to their imitation, in the old world. The love of Religious Liberty is a stronger sentiment, when fully excited, than an attachment to civil or political freedom. That freedom which the conscience demands, and which men feel bound by their hopes of salvation to contend for, can hardly fail to be attained. Conscience, in the cause of Religion, and the worship of the Deity, prepares .the mind to act, and to suffer beyond almost all other causes. It sometimes gives an impulse so irresistible, that no fetters of power or of opinion can withstand it. History instructs us that this love of Religious liberty, a compound sentiment in the breast of man, made up of the clearest sense of right, and the highest conviction of duty, is able to look the sternest despotism in the face, and with means apparently most inadequate, to shake principalities and powers. There is a boldness, a spirit of daring, in Religious reformers, not to be measured by the general rules which control men's purposes and actions. If the hand of power be laid upon it, this only seems to augment its force and its elasticity, and to cause its action to be more formidable and terrible. Human invention has devised nothing, human power has compassed nothing that can forcibly restrain it, when it breaks forth. Nothing can stop it, but to give way to it; nothing can check it, but indulgence. It loses its power· only when it has gained its object. ᐧ The principle of toleration, to which the world ᐧ has come so slowly, is‘ at once the most just and the most wise of all principles. Even when religious feeling takes a character of extravagance and enthusiasm, and seems to threaten the order of society, and shake the columns of the social edifice, its principal danger is in its restraint. If it be allowed indulgence and expansion like the elemental fires it only agitates and perhaps purifies the atmosphere, while its efforts to throw off restraint would burst the world asunder.

It is certain, that although many of them were Republicans in principle, we have no evidence that our New-England ancestors would have emigrated, as they did, from their own native country, become wanderers in Europe, and finally undertaken the ᐧ establishment of a colony here, merely from their dislike of the political systems of Europe. They fled not so much from the civil government, as from the Hierarchy, and the laws which enforced conformity to the Church Establishment. Mr. ᐧ Robinson had left England as early as sixteen hundred and eight, on account of the prosecutions for non-conformity, and had retired to Holland. He left England, from no disappointed ambition in affairs of state, from no regrets at the want of preferment in the Church, nor from any motive of distinction, or of gain. Uniformity in matters of Religion was pressed with such extreme rigour, that a voluntary exile seemed the most eligible mode of escaping from the penalties of non-compliance. The accession of Elizabeth had, it is true, quenched the fires of Smithfield, and put an·end to the easy acquisition of the crown of martyrdom. Her long reign had established the Reformation, but toleration was a virtue beyond her conception, and beyond the age. She left no example of it to her successor; and he was not of a character which rendered it probable that a sentiment either so wise or so liberal should originate with him. At the present period it seems incredible, that the learned, accomplished, unassuming, and inoffensive Robinson should neither be tolerated in his own peaceable mode of worship, in his own country, nor suffered quietly to depart from it. Yet such was the fact. He left his country

4

by stealth, that he might elsewhere enjoy those rights which ought to belong to men in all countries. The embarkation of the Pilgrims for Holland is deeply interesting, from its circumstances, and also as it marks the character of the times; independently of its connexion with names now incorporated with the history of Empire. The embarcation was intended to be in the night, that it might escape the notice of the officers of government. Great pains had been taken to secure boats, which should come undiscovered to the shore, and receive the fugitives; and frequent disappointments had been experienced in this respect. At length the appointed time came, bringing with it unusual severity of cold and rain. An unfrequented and barren heath, on the shores of Lincolnshire, was the selected spot, where the feet of the Pilgrims were to tread, for the last time, the land of their fathers.

The vessel which was to receive them, did not come until the next day, and in the mean time the little band was collected, and men and women and children and baggage were crowded together, in melancholy and distressed confusion. The sea was rough, and the women and children already sick, from their passage down the river to the place of embarcation. At length the wished for boat silently and fearfully approaches the shore, and men and women and children, shaking with fear and with cold, as many as the small vessel could bear, venture off on a dangerous sea. Immediately the advance of horses is heard from behind, armed men appear, and those not yet embarked are seized, and taken into custody. In the hurry of the moment, there had been no regard to the keeping together of families, in the first embarcation, and on account of the appearance of the horsemen, the boat never returned for the residue. Those who had got away, and those who had not, were in equal distress. A storm, of great violence, and long duration, arose at sea, which not only protracted the voyage, rendered distressing by the want of all those accommodations which the interruption of the embarcation had occasioned, but also forced the vessel out of her course, and menaced immediate shipwreck; while those on shore, when they

were dismissed from the custody of the officers
of justice, having no longer homes or houses to
retire to, and their friends and protectors being
already gone, became objects of necessary charity,
as well as of deep commiseration.

As this scene passes before us, we can hardly
forbear asking, whether this be a band of male-
factors and felons flying from justice? What are
their crimes, that they hide themselves in darkness?—To what punishment are they exposed,
that to avoid it, men, and women, and children,
thus encounter the surf of the North Sea, and the
terrors of a night storm? What induces this
armed pursuit, and this arrest of fugitives, of all
ages and both sexes?—Truth does not allow us
to answer these inquiries, in a manner that does
credit to the wisdom or the justice of the times.
This was not the flight of guilt, but of virtue.
It was an humble and peaceable religion, flying
from causeless oppression. It was conscience,
attempting to escape from the arbitrary rule of
the Stuarts. It was Robinson, and Brewster,
leading off their little band from their native soil,

at first to find shelter on the shores of the neighbouring continent, but ultimately to come hither;
and having surmounted all difficulties, and braved
a thousand dangers, to find here a place of refuge and of rest. Thanks be to God, that this
spot was honoured as the asylum of religious liberty. May its standard, reared here, remain forever!——May it rise up as high as heaven, till its
banner shall fan the air of both continents, and
wave as a glorious ensign of peace and security
to the nations!

The peculiar character, condition, and circumstances of the colonies which introduced civilization and an English race into New-England, af-
ford a most interesting and extensive topic of
discussion. On these much of our subsequent
character and fortune has depended. Their influence has essentially affected our whole history,
through the two centuries which have elapsed;
and as they have become intimately connected
with government, laws, and property, as well as
with our opinions on the subjects of religion and
civil liberty, that influence is likely to continue

to be felt through the centuries which shall succeed. Emigration from one region to another, and the emission of colonies to people countries more or less distant from the residence of the parent stock, are common incidents in the history of mankind ; but it has not often, perhaps never happened, that the establishment of colonies should be attempted, under circumstances, however beset with present difficulties and dangers, yet so favourable to ultimate success, and so conducive to magnificent results, as those which attended the first settlements on this part of the continent. In other instances, emigration has proceeded from a less exalted purpose, in a period of less general intelligence, or more without plan and by accident ; or under circumstances, physical and moral, less favourable to the expectation of laying a foundation for great public prosperity and future empire.

A great resemblance exists, obviously, between all the English colonies, established within the present limits of the United States ; but the occasion attracts our attention more immediately to those which took possession of New-England, and the peculiarities of these furnish a strong contrast with most other instances of colonization.

Among the ancient nations, the Greeks, no doubt, sent forth from their territories the greatest number of colonies. So numerous indeed were they, and so great the extent of space over which they were spread, that the parent country fondly and naturally persuaded herself, that by means of them she had laid a sure foundation for the universal civilization of the world. These establishments, from obvious causes, were most numerous in places most contiguous; yet they were found on the coasts of France, on the shores of the Euxine sea, in Africa, and even, as is alleged, on the borders of India. These emigrations appear to have been sometimes voluntary and sometimes compulsory; arising from the spontaneous enterprise of individuals, or the order and regulation of government. It was a common opinion with ancient writers, that they were undertaken in religious obedience to the commands of oracles; and it is probable that impressions of this sort might have had more or less influence; but it is probable, also, that on these occasions the oracles did not speak a language dissonant from the views and purposes of the state.

Political science among the Greeks seems never to have extended to the comprehension of a system, which should be adequate to the government of a great nation upon principles of liberty. They were accustomed only to the contemplation of small republics, and were led to consider an augmented population as incompatible with free institutions. The desire of a remedy for this supposed evil, and the wish to establish marts for trade, led the governments often to undertake the establishment of colonies as an affair of state expediency. Colonization and commerce, indeed, would naturally become objects of interest to an ingenious and enterprising people, inhabiting a territory closely circumscribed in its limits, and in no small part mountainous and sterile; while the islands of the adjacent seas, and the promontories and coasts of the neighbouring continents, by their mere proximity, strongly solicited the excited spirit of emigration. Such was this proximity, in many instances, that the new settlements appeared rather to be the mere extension of population over contiguous territory, than the establishment of distant colonies. In proportion as they were near to the parent state, they would be under its authority, and partake of its fortunes. The colony at Marseilles might perceive lightly, or not at all, the sway of Phocis ; while the islands in the Egean sea could hardly attain to independence of their Athenian origin. Many of these establishments took place at an early age ; and if there were defects in the governments of the parent states, the colonists did not possess philosophy or experience sufficient to correct such evils in their own institutions, even if they had not been, by other causes, deprived of the power. An immediate necessity, connected with the support of life, was the main and direct inducement to these undertakings, and there could hardly exist more than the hope of a successful imitation of institutions with which they were already acquainted, and of holding an equality with their neighbours, in the course of improvement. The laws and customs, both political and municipal, as well as the religious worship of the parent city, were transferred to the colony ; and the parent city herself, with all such of her colonies as were not too far remote for frequent intercourse, and common sentiments, would appear like a family of cities, more or less dependent, and more or less connected. We know how imperfect this system was, as a system of general politics, and what scope it gave to those mutual dissentions and conflicts which proved so fatal to Greece.

But it is more pertinent to our present purpose to observe, that nothing existed in the character of Grecian emigrations, or in the spirit and intelligence of the emigrants, likely to give a new and important direction to human affairs, or a new impulse to the human mind. Their motives were not high enough, their views were not sufficiently large and prospective. They went not forth, like our ancestors, to erect systems of more perfect civil liberty, or to enjoy a higher degree of religious freedom. Above all, there was nothing in the religion and learning of the age, that could either inspire high purposes, or give the ability to execute them. Whatever restraints on civil liberty, or whatever abuses in religious worship, existed at the time of our fathers' emigration, yet, even then, all was light in the moral and mental world, in comparison with its condition in most periods of the ancient states. The settlement of a new continent, in an age of progressive knowledge and improvement, could not but do more than merely enlarge the natural boundaries of the habitable world. It could not but do much more even than extend commerce and increase wealth among the human race. We see how this event has acted, how it must have acted, and wonder only why it did not act sooner, in the production of moral effects, on the state of human knowledge, the general tone of human sentiments, and the prospects of human happiness. It gave to civilized man not only a new continent to be inhabited and cultivated, and new seas to be explored; but it gave him also a new range for his thoughts, new objects for curiosity, and new excitements to knowledge and improvement.

Roman colonization resembled, far less than that of the Greeks, the original settlements of this country. Power and dominion were the objects of Rome, even in her colonial establishments. Her whole exterior aspect was for centuries hostile and terrific. She grasped at dominion, from India to Britain, and her measures of colonization partook of the character of her general system. Her policy was military, because her objects were power, ascendancy, and subjugation. Detachments of emigrants from Rome incorporated themselves with, and governed, the original inhabitants of conquered countries. She sent citizens where she had first sent soldiers; her law followed her sword. Her colonies were a sort of military establishment; so many advanced posts in the career of her dominion. A governor from Rome ruled the new colony with absolute sway, and often with unbounded rapacity. In Sicily, in Gaul, in Spain, and in Asia, the power of Rome prevailed, not nominally only, but really and effectually. Those who immediately exercised it were Roman; the tone and tendency of its administration, Roman. Rome herself continued to be the heart and centre of the great system which she had established. Extortion and rapacity, finding a wide and often rich field of action in the provinces, looked nevertheless to the banks of the Tiber, as the scene in which their ill-gotten treasures should be displayed; or if a spirit of more honest acquisition prevailed, the object, nevertheless, was ultimate enjoyment in Rome itself. If our own history, and our own times did not sufficiently expose the inherent and incurable evils of provincial government, we might see them portrayed, to our amazement, in the desolated and ruined provinces of the Roman empire. We might hear them, in a voice that terrifies us, in those strains of complaint and accusation, which the advocates of the provinces poured forth in the Roman Forum.—" *Quas res luxuries in flagitiis, crudelitas in suppliciis, avaritia in rapinis, superbia in contumeliis, efficere potuisset, eas omneis sese pertulisse.*"

As was to be expected, the Roman Provinces partook of the fortunes as well as of the sentiments and general character of the seat of em-

pire. They lived together with her, they flourished with her, and fell with her. The branches
were lopped away even before the vast and venerable trunk itself fell prostrate to the earth. Nothing had proceeded from her, which could support
itself, and bear up the name of its origin, when her
own sustaining arm should be enfeebled or with-
drawn. It was not given to Rome to see, either
at her zenith, or in her decline, a child of her
own, distant indeed, and independent of her control, yet speaking her language and inheriting
her blood, springing forward to a competition with
her own power, and a comparison with her own
great renown. She saw not a vast region of the
earth, peopled from her stock, full of states and
political communities, improving upon the models
of her institutions, and breathing in fuller measure
the spirit which she had breathed in the best
periods of her existence ; enjoying and extending
her arts and her literature ; rising rapidly from
political childhood to manly strength and independence ; her offspring, yet now her equal ;
unconnected with the causes which might affect
the duration of her own power and greatness ; of

common origin, but not linked to a common fate;
giving ample pledge, that her name should not
be forgotten, that her language should not cease
to be used among men; that whatsoever she had
done for human knowledge and human happiness, should be treasured up and preserved; that
the record of her existence, and her achievements,
should not be obscured although, in the inscruta-
ble purposes of Providence, it might be her desti-
ny to fall from opulence and splendour; although
the time might come, when darkness should
settle on all her hills; when foreign or domestic violence should overturn her altars and her
temples; when ignorance and despotism should
fill the places where Laws, and Arts, and Liberty had flourished; when the feet of barbarism
should trample on the tombs of her consuls,
and the walls of her senate house and forum
echo only to the voice of savage triumph. She
saw not this glorious vision, to inspire and fortify
her against the possible decay or downfal of her
power. Happy are they, who in our day may
behold it, if they shall contemplate it with the
sentiments which it ought to inspire!

The New-England colonies differ quite as widely from the Asiatic establishments of the modern
European Nations, as from the models of the
Ancient States. The sole object of those establishments was originally trade; although we
have seen, in one of them, the anomaly of a
mere trading company attaining a political character, disbursing revenues, and maintaining ar-
mies and fortresses, until it has extended its
control over seventy millions of people. Differing from these, and still differing more from
the New-England and North American Colonies,
are the European settlements in the West India
Islands. It is not strange, that when men's minds
were turned to the settlement of America, different objects should be proposed by those who
emigrated to the different regions of so vast a
country. Climate, soil, and condition were not
all equally favourable to all pursuits. In the
West Indies, the purpose of those who went
thither, was to engage in that species of agriculture, suited to the soil and climate, which seems
to bear more resemblance to commerce, than to
the hard and plain tillage of New England. The

great staples of these countries, being partly an
agricultural and partly a manufactured product,
and not being of the necessaries of life, become
the object of calculation, with respect to a profi-
table investment of capital, like any other enterprise of trade or manufacture. The more especially, as they require, by necessity or habit,
slave labour for their production, the capital
necessary to carry on the work of this production is more considerable. The West Indies
are resorted to, therefore, rather for the investment of capital, than for the purpose of sustaining life by personal labour. Such as possess a
considerable amount of capital, or such as choose
to adventure in commercial speculations without capital, can alone be fitted to be emigrants to
the islands. The agriculture of these regions,
as before observed, is a sort of commerce ; and
it is a species of employment, in which labour
seems to form an inconsiderable ingredient in the
productive causes ; since the portion of white
labour is exceedingly small, and slave labour is
rather more like profit on stock, or capital, than
labour properly so called. The individual who

contemplates an establishment of this kind, takes into the account the cost of the necessary number of slaves, in the same manner as he calculates the cost of the land. The uncertainty, too, of 'this species of employment, affords another ground of resemblance to commerce. Although gainful, on the whole, and in a series of years, it is often very disastrous for a single year, and as the capital is not readily invested in other pursuits, bad crops, or bad markets, not only affect the profits, but the capital itself. Hence the sudden depressions which take place in the value of such estates.

But the great and leading observation, relative to these establishments, remains to be made. It is, that the owners of the soil and of the capital seldom consider themselves *at home* in the colony. A very great portion of the soil itself is usually owned in the mother country ; a still greater is mortgaged for capital obtained there ; and, in general, those who are to derive an interest from the products, look to the parent country as the place for enjoyment of their wealth. The population is therefore constantly fluctuating. Nobody comes but to return. A constant succession of owners, agents, and factors takes place. Whatsoever the soil, forced by the unmitigated toil of slavery, can yield, is borne home to defray rents, and interest, and agencies; or to give the means of living in a better society. In such a state, it is evident that no spirit of permanent improvement is likely to spring up. Profits will not be invested with a distant view of benefiting posterity. Roads and canals will hardly be built; schools will not be founded; colleges will not be endowed. There will be few fixtures in society; no principles of utility or of elegance, planted now, with the hope of being developed and expanded hereafter. Profit, immediate profit, must be the principal active spring in the social system. There may be many particular exceptions to these general remarks, but the outline of the whole, is such as is here drawn.

Another most important consequence of such a state of things is, that no idea of independence of the parent country is likely to arise; unless indeed it should spring up in a form, that would threaten universal desolation. The inhabitants have no strong attachment to the place which they inhabit. The hope of a great portion of them, is to leave it; and their great desire, to leave it soon. However useful they may be to the parent state, how much soever they may add to the conveniences and luxuries of life, these colonies are not favoured spots, for the expansion of the human mind, for the progress of permanent improvement, or for sowing the seeds of future independent empire.

Different, indeed, most widely different, from all these instances of emigration and plantation, were the condition, the purposes, and the prospects of our Fathers, when they established their infant colony upon this spot. They came hither to a land from which they were never to return. Hither they had brought, and here they were to fix, their hopes, their attachments, and their objects. Some natural tears they shed, as they left the pleasant abodes of their fathers, and some emotions they suppressed, when the white cliffs of their native country, now seen for the last time, grew dim to their sight. They were acting however upon a resolution not to be changed. With whatever stifled regrets, with whatever occasional hesitation, with whatever appalling apprehensions, which might sometimes arise with force to shake the firmest purpose, they had yet committed themselves to heaven, and the elements; and a thousand leagues of water soon interposed to separate them forever from the region which gave them birth. A new existence awaited them here; and when they saw these shores, rough, cold, barbarous, and barren as then they were, they beheld their country. That mixed and strong feeling, which we call love of country, and which is, in general, never extinguished in the heart of man, grasped and embraced its proper object here. Whatever constitutes *country*, except the earth and the sun, all the moral causes of affection and attachment, which operate upon the heart, they had brought with them to their new abode. Here were now their families and friends; their homes, and their property. Before they reached the shore, they had established the elements of a social system, and at a much earlier period had settled their forms of religious worship. At the moment of their land-

ing, therefore, they possessed institutions of government, and institutions of religion : and friends
and families, and social and religious institutions,
established by consent, founded on choice and
preference, how nearly do these fill up our whole
idea of country !—The morning that beamed on
the first night of their repose, saw the Pilgrims
already established in their country. There were
political institutions, and civil liberty, and religious
worship. Poetry has fancied nothing, in the wander-
ings of heroes, so distinct and characteristic. Here
was man, indeed, unprotected, and unprovided for,
on the shore of a rude and fearful wilderness ;
but it was politic, intelligent and educated man.
Every thing was civilized but the physical world.
Institutions containing in substance all that ages
had done for human government, were established
in a forest. Cultivated mind was to act on unculti-
vated nature ; and, more than all, a government,
and a country, were to commence, with the very
first foundations laid under the divine light of the
christian religion. Happy auspices of a happy
futurity ! Who would wish, that his country's
existence had otherwise begun ?—Who would de-

sire the power of going back to the ages of fable?
Who would wish for an origin, obscured in the
darkness of antiquity?—Who would wish for
other emblazoning of his country's heraldry,
or other ornaments of her genealogy, than to be
able to say, that her first existence was with intelligence; her first breath the inspirations of liberty; her first principle the truth of divine religion?

Local attachments and sympathies would ere
long spring up in the breasts of our ancestors,
endearing to them the place of their refuge.
Whatever natural objects are associated with interesting scenes and high efforts, obtain a hold
on human feeling, and demand from the heart a
sort of recognition and regard. This Rock soon
became hallowed in the esteem of the Pilgrims,
and these hills grateful to their sight. Neither
they nor their children were again to till the soil
of England, nor again to traverse the seas which
surrounded her. But here was a new sea, now
open to their enterprise, and a new soil, which
had not failed to respond gratefully to their labo-

rious industry, and which was already assuming a a robe of verdure. Hardly had they provided shelter for the living, ere they were summoned to erect sepulchres for the dead. The ground had become sacred, by enclosing the remains of some of their companions and connexions. A parent, a child, a husband or a wife, had gone the way of all flesh, and mingled with the dust of New-England. We naturally look with strong emotions to the spot, though it be a wilderness, where the ashes of those we have loved repose. Where the heart has laid down what it loved most, it is desirous of laying itself down. No sculptured marble, no enduring monument, no honourable inscription, no ever burning taper that would drive away the darkness of death, can soften our sense of the reality of mortality, and hallow to our feelings the ground which is to cover us, like the consciousness that we shall sleep, dust to dust, with the objects of our affections.

In a short time other causes sprung up to bind the Pilgrims with new cords to their chosen land.

Children were born, and the hopes of future generations arose, in the spot of their new habitation.
The second generation found this the land of their
nativity, and saw that they were bound to its fortunes. They beheld their father's graves around
them, and while they read the memorials of their
toils and labours, they rejoiced in the inheritance
which they found bequeathed to them.

Under the influence of these causes, it was
to be expected, that an interest and a feeling should arise here, entirely different from the
interest and feeling of mere Englishmen ; and
all the subsequent history of the colonies proves
this to have actually and gradually taken place.
With a general acknowledgment of the su-
premacy of the British crown, there was, from
the first, a repugnance to an entire submis-
sion to the control of British legislation. The
colonies stood upon their charters, which as
they contended, exempted them from the ordinary power of the British parliament, and au-
thorised them to conduct their own concerns by
their own councils. They utterly resisted the

7

notion that they were to be ruled by the mere
authority of the government at home, and would
not endure even that their own charter governments should be established on the other side of
the Atlantic. It was not a controling or protect-
ing board in England, but a government of their
own, and existing immediately within their limits,
which could satisfy their wishes. It was easy
to foresee, what we know also to have happened,
that the first great cause of collision and jealousy
would be, under the notion of political economy
then and still prevalent in Europe, an attempt on
the part of the mother country to monopolize the
trade of the colonies. Whoever has looked
deeply into the causes which produced our revolution, has found, if I mistake not, the original
principle far back in this claim, on the part of
England, to monopolize our trade, and a continued effort on the part of the colonies to resist or
evade that monopoly; if indeed it be not still
more just and philosophical to go farther back,
and to consider it decided, that an independent
government must arise here, the moment it was
ascertained that an English colony, such as land-

ed in this place, could sustain itself against the dangers which surrounded it, and, with other similar establishments, overspread the land with an English population. Accidental causes retarded at times, and at times accelerated the progress of the controversy. The colonies wanted strength, and time gave it to them. They required measures of strong and palpable injustice on the part of the mother country, to justify resistance ; the early part of the late King's reign furnished them. They needed spirits of high order, of great daring, of long foresight and of commanding power, to seize the favouring occasion to strike a blow, which should sever, forever, the tie of colonial dependence ; and these spirits were found, in all the extent which that or any crisis could demand, in Otis, Adams, Hancock, and the other immediate authors of our independence. Still it is true, that for a century, causes had been in operation tending to prepare things for this great result. In the year 1660 the English act of Navigation was passed ; the first and grand object of which seems to have been to secure to England the whole trade with her plantations. It was provided, by that act, that none but English ships should transport American produce over the ocean ; and that the principal articles of that produce should be allowed to be sold only in the markets of the mother country. Three years afterwards another law was passed, which enacted, that such commodities as the colonies might wish to purchase, should be bought only in the markets of the mother country. Severe rules were prescribed to enforce the provisions of these laws, and heavy penalties imposed on all who should violate them. In the subsequent years of the same reign, other statutes were passed, to reinforce these statutes, and other rules prescribed, to secure a compliance with these rules. In this manner was the trade, to and from the colonies, tied up, almost to the exclusive advantage of the parent country. But laws, which rendered the interest of a whole people subordinate to that of another people, were not likely to execute themselves ; nor was it easy to find many on the spot, who could be depended upon for carrying them into execution. In fact, these laws were more or less evaded, or resisted, in all the colonies. To enforce them was the constant endeavour of the government at home ; to prevent or elude their operation, the perpetual object here. " The laws of navigation," says a living British writer, " were no where so openly disobeyed and contemned, as in New-England." " The People of Massachusetts Bay," he adds, " were from the first disposed to act as if independent of the mother country, and having a Governor and magistrates of their own choice, it was difficult to enforce any regulation which came from the English parliament, adverse to their interests." To provide more effectually for the execution of these laws, we know that courts of admiralty were afterwards established by the crown, with power to try revenue causes, as questions of admiralty, upon the construction, given by the crown lawyers, to an act of parliament ;—a great departure from the ordinary principles of English jurisprudence, but which has been maintained, nevertheless, by the force of habit and precedent, and is adopted in our own existing systems of government.

" There lie," says another English writer, whose connexion with the Board of Trade has enabled him to ascertain many facts connected with colonial history,—" There lie among the documents in the board of trade and paper office, the most satisfactory proofs, from the epoch of the English revolution in 1688, throughout every reign, and during every administration, of the settled purpose of the colonies to acquire direct independence and positive sovereignty." Perhaps this may be stated somewhat too strongly; but it cannot be denied, that from the very nature of the establishments here, and from the general character of the measures respecting their concerns, early adopted, and steadily pursued by the English government, a division of the empire was the natural and necessary result to which every thing tended.

I have dwelt on this topic, because it seems to me, that the peculiar original character of the New-England colonies, and certain causes coeval with their existence, have had a strong and decided influence on all their subsequent history, and especially on the great event of the Revolution. Whoever would write our history, and would understand and explain early transactions, should comprehend the nature and force of the feeling which I have endeavoured to describe. As a son, leaving the house of his father for his own, finds, by the order of nature, and the very law of his being, nearer and dearer objects around which his affections circle, while his attachment to the parental roof becomes moderated, by degrees, to a composed regard, and an affectionate remembrance; so our ancestors, leaving their native land, not without some violence to the feelings of nature and affection, yet in time found here, a new circle of engagements, interests, and affections; a feeling, which more and more encroached upon the old, till an undivided sentiment, *that this was their country,* occupied the heart; and patriotism, shutting out from its embraces the parent realm, became *local* to America.

Some retrospect of the century which has now elapsed, is among the duties of the occasion. It must, however, necessarily be imperfect, to be compressed within the limits of a single discourse. I shall content myself, therefore, with taking notice of a few of the leading, and most important, occurrences, which have distinguished the period.

When the first century closed, the progress of the country appeared to have been considerable ; notwithstanding that, in comparison with its subsequent advancement, it now seems otherwise. A broad and lasting foundation had been laid : excellent institutions had been established ; much of the prejudices of former times had become removed ; a more liberal and catholic spirit on subjects of religious concern had begun to extend itself, and many things conspired to give promise of increasing future prosperity. Great men had arisen in public life and the liberal professions. The Mathers, father and son, were then sinking low in the western horizon ; Leverett, the learned, the accomplished, the excellent Leverett, was about to withdraw his brilliant and useful light. In Pemberton, great hopes had been suddenly extinguished, but Prince and Colman, were in our sky; and the crepuscular light had begun to flash along the East, of a great luminary which was about to appear; and which was to mark the age with his own name, as the age of Franklin.

The bloody Indian wars, which harrassed the people for a part of the first century; the restrictions on the trade of the Colonies—added to the discouragements inherently belonging to all forms of colonial government; the distance from Europe, and the small hope of immediate profit to adventurers, are among the causes which had contributed to retard the progress of population. Perhaps it may be added, also, that during the period of the civil wars in England, and the reign of Cromwell, many persons, whose religious opinions and religious temper might, under other circumstances have induced them to join the New-England colonists, found reasons to remain in England; either on account of active occupation in the scenes which were passing, or of an anticipation of the enjoyment, in their own country, of a form of government, civil and religious, accommodated to their views and principles. The violent measures, too, pursued against the Colonies in the reign of Charles the second, the mockery of a trial, and the forfeiture of the Charters, were serious evils. And during the open violences of the short reign of James the second, and the tyranny of Andros, as the venerable historian of Connecticut observes, "*All the motives to great actions, to industry, economy, enterprize, wealth, and population, were in a manner annihilated. A general inactivity and languishment pervaded the public body. Liberty, property, and every thing which ought to be dear to men, every day grew more and more insecure.*"

With the revolution in England, a better prospect had opened on this country, as well as on that. The joy had been as great, at that event, and far more universal in *New*, than in *Old* England. A new Charter had been granted to Massachusetts, which, although it did not confirm to her inhabitants all their former privileges, yet relieved them from great evils and embarrassments, and promised future security.   More than all, perhaps, the revolution in England, had done good to the *general* cause of liberty and justice. A blow had been struck, in favour of the rights and liberties, not of England alone, but of descendants and kinsmen of England, all over the world. Great political truths had been established. The champions of liberty had been successful in a fearful and perilous conflict.   Somers, and Cavendish, and Jekyl, and Howard, had triumphed in one of the most noble causes ever undertaken by men.   A revolution had been made upon principle.   A monarch had been dethroned, for violating the original compact between King and People.   The rights of the people to partake in the government, and to limit the monarch by fundamental rules of government, had been maintained ; and however unjust the government of England might afterwards be, towards other governments or towards her colonies, she had ceased to be governed herself, by the arbitrary maxims of the Stuarts.

New-England had submitted to the violence of James the second, not longer than Old England.

Not only was it reserved to Massachusetts, that on her soil should be acted the first scene of that great revolutionary Drama, which was to take place near a century afterwards, but the English revolution itself, as far as the Colonies were concerned, commenced in Boston. A direct and forcible resistance to the authority of James the second, was the seizure and imprisonment of Andros, in April 1689. The pulse of Liberty beat as high in the extremities, as at the heart. The vigorous feeling of the Colony burst out, before it was known how the parent country would finally conduct itself. The King's representative, Sir Edmund Andros, was a prisoner in the Castle at Boston, before it was or could be known, that the King himself had ceased to exercise his full dominion on the English throne.

Before it was known here, whether the invasion of the Prince of Orange would or could prove successful; as soon only as it was known that it had been undertaken, the people of Massachusetts, at the imminent hazard of their lives and fortunes, had accomplished the revolution as far as respected themselves. It is probable, that, reasoning on general principles, and the known attachment of the English people to their constitution and liberties, and their deep and fixed dislike of the King's religion and politics, the people of New-England expected a catastrophe fatal to the power of the reigning Prince. Yet, it was not either certain enough, or near enough, to come to their aid against the authority of the crown, in that crisis which had arrived, and in which they trusted to put themselves, relying on God, and on their own courage. There were spirits in Massachusetts, congenial with the spirits of the distinguished friends of the revolution in England. There were those, who were fit to associate with the boldest asserters of civil liberty; and Mather himself, then in England, was not unworthy to be ranked with those sons of the church, whose firmness and spirit, in resisting kingly encroachment in religion, entitled them to the gratitude of their own and succeeding ages.

The Second Century opened upon New-England under circumstances, which evinced, that much had already been accomplished, and that still better prospects, and brighter hopes, were before her. She had laid, deep and strong, the foundations of her society. Her religious principles were firm, and her moral habits exemplary. Her public schools had begun to diffuse widely the elements of knowledge ; and the College, under the excellent and acceptable administration of Leverett, had been raised to a high degree of credit and usefulness.

The commercial character of the country, notwithstanding all discouragements, had begun to display itself, and *five hundred vessels*, then belonging to Massachusetts, placed her in relation to commerce, thus early, at the head of the colonies. An author who wrote very near the close of the first century says ; " New-England is almost deserving that *noble name ;* so mightily hath it increased ; and from a small settlement, at first, is now become a *very populous* and *flourishing* government. The *capital city*, Boston, is a place of *great wealth and trade ;* and by much the largest of any in the English empire of Ameri-

ca ; and not exceeded but by few cities, perhaps two or three, in all the American world.

But, if our ancestors at the close of the first
century, could look back with joy, and even
admiration, at the progress of the country; what
emotions must we not feel, when, from the point
in which we stand, we also look back and run
along the events of the century which has now
closed ? The country, which then, as we have
seen, was thought deserving of a " noble name ;"
which then had " mightily increased," and become " very populous ;" what was it, in comparison with what our eyes behold it ? At that
period, a very great proportion of its inhabitants
lived in the Eastern section of Massachusetts
proper, and in this colony. In Connecticut, there
were towns along the coast, some of them respectable, but in the interior, all was a wilderness
beyond Hartford. On Connecticut river, settlements had proceeded as far up as Deerfield, and
fort Dummer had been built, near where is now
the South line of New-Hampshire. In New-Hampshire, no settlement was then begun thirty miles

from the mouth of Piscataqua river, and, in what is now Maine, the inhabitants were confined to the coast. The aggregate of the whole population of New-England did not exceed one hundred and sixty thousand. Its present amount is probably one million seven hundred thousand. Instead of being confined to its former limits, her population has rolled backward and filled up the spaces included within her actual local boundaries. Not this only, but it has overflowed those boundaries, and the waves of emigration have pressed, farther and farther, toward the west. The Alleghany has not checked it ; the banks of the Ohio have been covered with it. New-England farms, houses, villages, and churches spread over, and adorn the immense extent from the Ohio to Lake Erie ; and stretch along, from the Alleghany, onwards beyond the Miamies, and towards the Falls of St. Anthony. Two thousand miles, westward from the rock where their fathers landed, may now be found the sons of the Pilgrims ; cultivating smiling fields, rearing towns and villages, and cherishing, we trust, the patrimonial blessings of wise institutions, of liberty, and religion. The world has seen nothing like this. Regions large enough to be empires, and which, half a century ago, were known only as remote and unexplored wildernesses, are now teeming with population, and prosperous in all the great concerns of life ; in good governments, the means of subsistence, and social happiness. It may be safely asserted, that there are now more than a *million* of people, descendants of New-England ancestry, living free and happy, in regions, which hardly sixty years ago, were tracts of unpenetrated forest. Nor do rivers, or mountains, or seas resist the progress of industry and enterprise. Ere long, the sons of the Pilgrims will be on the shores of the Pacific. The imagination hardly keeps up with the progress of population, improvement, and civilization.

It is now five and forty years, since the growth and rising glory of America were portrayed, in the English parliament, with inimitable beauty, by the most consummate orator of modern times. Going back somewhat more than half a century, and describing our progress, as foreseen, from that point, by his amiable friend Lord Bathurst, then living, he spoke of the wonderful progress which America had made, during the period of a single human life. There is no American heart, I imagine, that does not glow, both with conscious patriotic pride, and admiration for one of the happiest efforts of eloquence, so often as the vision, of " that little speck, scarce visible in the mass of national interest, a small seminal principle, rather than a formed body," and the progress of its astonishing development and growth, are recalled to the recollection. But a stronger feeling might be produced, if we were able to take up this prophetic description where he left it ; and placing ourselves at the point of time in which he was speaking, to set forth with equal felicity, the subsequent progress of the country. There is yet among the living a most distinguished and venerable name, a descendant of the Pilgrims ; one who has been attended through life by a great and fortunate genius ; a man illustrious by his own great merits, and favoured of Heaven in the long continuation of his years. The time when the English orator was thus speaking of

America, preceded, but by a few days, the actual
opening of the revolutionary Drama at Lexing-
ton. He to whom I have alluded, then at the
age of forty, was among the most zealous and able
defenders of the violated rights of his country.
He seemed already to have filled a full measure
of public service, and attained an honorable fame.
The moment was full of difficulty and danger, and
big with events of immeasurable importance.
The country was on the very brink of a civil war,
of which no man could foretell the duration or
the result. Something more than a courageous
hope, or characteristic ardour, would have been
necessary to impress the glorious prospect on his
belief, if, at that moment, before the sound of the
first shock of actual war had reached his ears,
some attendant spirit had opened to him the
vision of the future ; if it had said to him, " The
blow is struck, and America is severed from England forever !" if it had informed him, that he
himself, the next annual revolution of the sun,
should put his own hand to the great Instrument
of Independence, and write his name where all
nations should behold it, and all time should not

efface it ; that ere long he himself should maintain the interest and represent the sovereignty of his new-born Country, in the proudest courts of Europe ; that he should one day exercise her supreme magistracy ; that he should yet live to behold ten millions of fellow citizens paying him the homage of their deepest gratitude and kindest affections ; that he should see distinguished talent and high public trust resting where his name rested ; that he should even see with his own unclouded eyes, the close of the second century of New-England, who had begun life almost with its commencement, and lived through nearly half the whole history of his country ; and that on the morning of this auspicious day, he should be found in the political councils of his native state, revising, by the light of experience, that system of government, which forty years before he had assisted to frame and establish ; and great and happy as he should then behold his country, there should be nothing in prospect to cloud the scene, nothing to check the ardour of that confident and patriotic hope, which should glow in his bosom to the end of his long protracted and happy life.

It would far exceed the limits of this discourse, even to mention the principal events in the civil and political history of New-England during the century; the more so, as for the last half of the period, that history has been, most happily, closely interwoven with the general history of the United States. New-England bore an honorable part in the wars which took place between England and France. The capture of Louisburg gave her a character for military achievement; and in the war which terminated with the peace of 1763, her exertions on the frontiers were of most essential service as well to the mother country as to all the colonies.

In New-England the war of the revolution commenced. I address those who remember the memorable 19th of April 1775; who shortly after saw the burning spires of Charlestown; who beheld the deeds of Prescott, and heard the voice of Putnam, amidst the storm of war, and saw the generous Warren fall, the first distinguished victim in the cause of liberty. It would be superfluous to say, that no portion of the country did more than the states of New-England, to bring the revolutionary struggle to a successful issue. It is scarcely less to her credit, that she saw early the necessity of a closer union of the states, and gave an efficient and indispensable aid to the establishment and organization of the federal government.

Perhaps we might safely say, that a new spirit, and a new excitement began to exist here, about the middle of the last century. To whatever causes it may be imputed, there seems then to have commenced a more rapid improvement. The colonies had attracted more of the attention of the mother country, and some renown in arms had been acquired. Lord Chatham was the first English minister who attached high importance to these possessions of the crown, and who foresaw any thing of their future growth and extension. His opinion was, that the great rival of England was chiefly to be feared as a maritime and commercial power, and to drive her out of North America, and deprive her of her West India possessions was a leading object in his policy. He dwelt often on the fisheries, as nurseries for British seamen, and the colonial trade, as furnishing them employment. The war, conducted by him with so much vigour, terminated in a Peace, by which Canada was ceded to England. The effect of this was immediately visible in the New-England colonies; for the fear of Indian hostilities on the frontiers being now happily removed, settlements went on with an activity before that time altogether unprecedented, and public affairs wore a new and encouraging aspect. Shortly after this fortunate termination of the French war, the interesting topics connected with the taxation of America by the British Parliament began to be discussed, and the attention and all the faculties of the people drawn towards them. There is perhaps no portion of our history more full of interest than the period from 1760 to the actual commencement of the war. The progress of opinion, in this period, though less known, is not less important, than the progress of arms afterwards. Nothing deserves more consideration than those events and discussions which affected the public sentiment, and settled the Revolution in men's minds, before hostilities openly broke out.

Internal improvement followed the establishment, and prosperous commencement, of the present government. More has been done for roads, canals, and other public works, within the last thirty years, than in all our former history. In the first of these particulars, few countries excel the New-England States. The astonishing increase of their navigation and trade is known to every one, and now belongs to the history of our national wealth.

We may flatter ourselves, too, that literature and taste have not been stationary, and that some advancement has been made in the elegant, as well as in the useful arts.

The nature and constitution of society and government, in this country, are interesting topics, to which I would devote what remains of the time allowed to this occasion. Of our system of government, the first thing to be said, is, that it is

really and practically a free system. It originates
entirely with the people, and rests on no other
foundation than their assent. To judge of its actual operation, it is not enough to look merely at
the form of its construction. The practical character of government depends often on a variety
of considerations, besides the abstract frame of
its constitutional organization. Among these, are
the condition and tenure of property ; the laws
regulating its alienation and descent ; the presence
or absence of a military power ; an armed or un-
armed yeomanry; the spirit of the age, and the
degree of general intelligence. In these respects
it cannot be denied, that the circumstances of this
country are most favourable to the hope of maintaining the government of a great nation on principles entirely popular. In the absence of military power, the nature of government must
essentially depend on the manner in which property is holden and distributed. There is a natural influence belonging to property, whether it
exists in many hands or few ; and it is on the rights
of property, that both despotism and unrestrained
popular violence ordinarily commence their at-

10

tacks. Our ancestors began their system of government here, under a condition of comparative equality, in regard to wealth, and their early laws were of a nature to favour and continue this equality.* A republican form of government rests, not more on political Constitutions, than on those laws which regulate the descent and transmission of property.——Governments like ours could not have been maintained, where property was holden according to the principles of the feudal·system ; nor, on the other hand, could the feudal Constitution possibly exist with us. Our New-England ancestors brought hither no great capitals, from Europe ; and if they had, there was nothing productive, in which they could have been ·invested. They left behind them the

---

* The contents of several of the following pages will be found also in the printed account of the proceedings of the Massachusetts convention, in some remarks made by the author a few days before the delivery of this discourse. As those remarks were originally written for this discourse, it was thought proper not to omit them, in the publication, notwithstanding this circumstance.

whole feudal policy of the other continent. They broke away, at once, from the system of military service, established in the dark ages, and which continues, down even to the present time, more or less to affect the condition of property all over Europe. They came to a new country. There were, as yet, no lands yielding rent, and no tenants rendering service. The whole soil was unreclaimed from barbarism. They were themselves, either from their original condition, or from the necessity of their common interest, nearly on a general level, in respect to property. Their situation demanded a parcelling out and division of the lands; and it may be fairly said, that this necessary act *fixed the future frame and form of their government.* The character of their political institutions was determined by the fundamental laws respecting property. The laws rendered estates divisible among sons and daughters. The right of primogeniture, at first limited, and curtailed, was afterwards abolished. The property was all freehold. The entailment of estates, long trusts, and the other processes for fettering and tying up inheritances, were not applicable to the condition of society, and seldom made use of. On the contrary, alienation of the land was every way facilitated, even to the sub-jecting of it to every species of debt. The establishment of public registries, and the simplici-ty of our forms of conveyance, have greatly facili-tated the change of real estate, from one proprie-tor to another. The consequence of all these causes has been, a great subdivision of the soil, and a great equality of condition ; the true basis most certainly of a popular government.—" If the people," says Harrington, " hold three parts in four of the territory, it is plain there can nei-ther be any single person nor nobility able to dis-pute the government with them ; in this case, therefore, *except force be interposed*, they govern themselves."

The history of other nations may teach us how favourable to public liberty is the division of the soil into small freeholds, and a system of laws, of which the tendency is, without violence or injus-tice, to produce and to preserve a degree of equality of property. It has been estimated, if I mistake not, that about the time of Henry the VII., four fifths of the land in England, was holden by the great barons and ecclesiastics. The effects of a growing commerce soon afterwards began to break in on this state of things, and before the revolution in 1688 a vast change had been wrought. It may be thought probable, that, for the last half century, the process of subdivision in England,has been retarded, if not re versed; that the great weight of taxation has compelled many of the lesser freeholders to dispose of their estates, and to seek employment in the army and navy; in the professions of civil life; in commerce or in the colonies. The effect of this on the British Constitution cannot but be most unfavourable. A few large estates grow larger; but the number of those who have no estates also increases; and there may be danger, lest the inequality of property become so great, that those who possess it may be dispossessed by force; in other words, that the government may be overturned.

A most interesting experiment of the effect of

a subdivision of property on government, is now making in France. It is understood, that the law regulating the transmission of property, in that country, now divides it, real and personal, among all the children, equally, both sons and daughters; and that there is, also, a very great restraint on the power of making dispositions of property by will. It has been supposed, that the effects of this might probably be, in time, to break up the soil into such small subdivisions, that the proprietors would be too *poor* to resist the encroachments of executive power. I think far otherwise. What is lost in individual wealth, will be more than gained, in numbers, in intelligence, and in a sympathy of sentiment. If indeed, only one, or a few landholders were to resist the crown, like the barons of England, they must, of course, be great and powerful landholders with multitudes of retainers, to promise success. But if the proprietors of a given extent of territory are summoned to resistance, there is no reason to believe that such resistance would be less forcible, or less successful, because the number of such proprietors should be great. Each would perceive his own importance, and his own interest, and would feel that natural elevation of character which the consciousness of property inspires. A common sentiment would unite all, and numbers would not only add strength, but excite enthusiasm. It is true, that France possesses a vast military force, under the direction of an hereditary executive government; and military power, it is possible, may overthrow any government. It is, in vain, however, in this period of the world, to look for security against military power, to the arm of the great landholders. That notion is derived from a state of things long since past ; a state in which a feudal baron, with his retainers, might stand against the sovereign, who was himself but the greatest baron, and his retainers. But at present, what could the richest landholder do, against one regiment of disciplined troops ? Other securities, therefore, against the prevalence of military power must be provided. Happily for us, we are not so situated as that any purpose of national defence requires, ordinarily and constantly, such a military force as might seriously endanger our liberties.

In respect, however, to the recent law of succession in France, to which I have alluded, I would, presumptuously perhaps, hazard a conjecture, that if the government do not change the law, the law, in half a century, will change the government; and that this change will be not in favour of the power of the crown, as some European writers have supposed, but against it. Those writers only reason upon what they think correct general principles, in relation to this subject. They acknowledge a want of experience. Here we have had that experience; and we know that a multitude of small proprietors, acting with intelligence, and that enthusiasm which a common cause inspires, constitute not only a formidable, but an invincible power.

The true principle of a free and popular government would seem to be, so to construct it, as to give to all, or at least to a very great majority, an interest in its preservation: to found it, as other things are founded, on men's interest. The stability of government. requires that those who desire its continuance should be more powerful

than those who desire its dissolution. This power-
er, of course, is not always to be measured by
mere numbers.——Education, wealth, talents, are
all parts and elements of the general aggregate of
power ; but numbers, nevertheless, constitute
ordinarily the most important consideration, unless indeed there be *a military force*, in the hands
of the few, by which they can control the many.
In this country we have actually existing systems of
government, in the maintenance of which, it should
seem, a great majority, both in numbers and in
other means of power and influence, must see
their interest. But this state of things is not
brought about solely by written political constitutions, or the mere manner of organizing the
government ; but also by the laws which regulate
the descent and transmission of property. The
freest government, if it could exist, would not be
long acceptable, if the tendency of the laws were
to create a rapid accumulation of property in few
hands, and to render the great mass of the population dependent and pennyless: In such a case, the
popular power would be likely to break in upon the
rights of property, or else the influence of property

to limit and control the exercise of popular power.;
—Universal suffrage, for example, could not long
exist in a community, where there was great inequality of property. The holders of estates
would be obliged in such case, either, in some
way, to restrain the right of suffrage ; or else
such right of suffrage would, long before, divide the
property. In the nature of things, those who
have not property, and see their neighbours possess much more than they think them to need,
cannot be favourable to laws made for the pro-
tection of property. When this class becomes
numerous, it grows clamorous. It looks on property as its prey and plunder, and is naturally
ready, at all times, for violence and revolution.

It would seem, then, to be the part of political
wisdom, to found government on property ; and to
establish such distribution of property, by the
laws which regulate its transmission and alienation, as to interest the great majority of society
in the support of the government. This is, I
imagine, the true theory and the actual practice
of our republican institutions. With property

divided, as we have it, no other government than that of a republic could be maintained, even were we foolish enough to desire it. There is reason, therefore, to expect a long continuance of our systems. Party and passion, doubtless, may prevail at times, and much temporary mischief be done. Even modes and forms may be changed, and perhaps for the worse. But a great revolution, in regard to property, must take place, before our governments can be moved from their republican basis, unless they be violently struck off by military power. The people possess the property, more emphatically than it could ever be said of the people of any other country, and they can have no interest to overturn a government which protects that property by equal laws.

Let it not be supposed, that this state of things possesses too strong tendencies towards the production of a dead and uninteresting level in society. Such tendencies are sufficiently counteracted by the infinite diversities in the characters and fortunes of individuals. Talent, activity, industry, and enterprize tend at all times to produce

inequality and distinction; and there is room
still for the accumulation of wealth, with its
great advantages, to all reasonable and useful
extent. It has been often urged against the state
of society in America, that it furnishes no class of
men of fortune and leisure. This may be partly
true, but it is not entirely so, and the evil, if it be
one, would affect rather the progress of taste
and literature, than the general prosperity of the
people. But the promotion of taste and literature cannot be primary objects of political institutions; and if they could, it might be doubted,
whether, in the long course of things, as much is not
gained by a wide diffusion of general knowledge,
as is lost by abridging the number of those whom
fortune and leisure enable to devote themselves ex-
clusively to scientific and literary pursuits. However this may be, it is to be considered that it is
the spirit of our system to be equal, and general,
and if there be particular disadvantages incident
to this, they are far more than counterbalanc-
ed by the benefits which weigh against them.
The important concerns of society are generally
conducted, in all countries, by the men of busi-
ness and practical ability; and even in matters of

taste and literature, the advantages of mere leisure are liable to be over-rated. If there exist adequate means of education, and the love of letters be excited, that love will find its way to the object of its desire, through the crowd and pressure of the most busy society.

Connected with this division of property, and the consequent participation of the great mass of people, in its possession and enjoyments, is the system of representation, which is admirably accommodated to our condition, better understood among us, and more familiarly and extensively practised, in the higher and in the lower departments of government, than it has been with any other people. Great facility has been given to this in New-England by the early division of the country into townships or small districts, in which all concerns of local police are regulated, and in which representatives to the Legislature are elected. Nothing can exceed the utility of these little bodies. They are so many Councils, or Parliaments, in which common interests are discussed, and useful knowledge acquired and communicated.

The division of governments into departments,
and the division, again, of the legislative depart-
ment into two chambers, are essential provisions
in our systems. This last, although not new in
itself, yet seems to be new in its application to
governments wholly popular. The Grecian Republics, it is plain, knew nothing of it; and in
Rome, the check and balance of legislative power, such as it was, lay between the people, and the
senate. Indeed few things are more difficult than
to ascertain accurately the true nature and construction of the Roman Commonwealth. The relative power of the senate and the people, the
Consuls and the Tribunes, appears not to have
been at all times the same, nor at any time accurately defined or strictly observed. Cicero, indeed,
describes to us an admirable arrangement of political power, and a balance of the constitution, in
that beautiful passage, in which he compares the
democracies of Greece with the Roman Commonwealth. " *O morem preclarum, disciplinamque,
quam a majoribus accepimus, si quidem teneremus!
sed nescio quo pacto jam de manibus elabitur. Nul-
lam enim illi nostri sapientissimi et sanctissimi viri*

vim concionis esse voluerunt, quae scisseret plebs, aut quae populus juberet ; summota concione, distributis partibus, tributim, et centuriatim, descriptis ordinibus, classibus, aetatibus, auditis auctoribus, re multos dies promulgata et cognita, juberi vetarique voluerunt. Graecorum autem totae respublicae sedentis concionis temeritate administrantur."

But at what time this wise system existed in this perfection at Rome, no proofs remain to show. Her constitution, originally framed for a monarchy, never seemed to be adjusted, in its several parts, after the expulsion of the kings. Liberty there was, but it was a disputatious, an uncertain, an ill-secured liberty. The patrician and plebeian orders, instead of being matched and joined, each in its just place and proportion, to sustain the fabric of the state, were rather like hostile powers, in perpetual conflict. With us, an attempt has been made, and so far not without success, to divide representation into Chambers, and by difference of age, character, qualification or mode of election, to establish salutary checks, in governments altogether elective.

Having detained you so long with these observations, I must yet advert to another most interesting topic, the FREE SCHOOLS. In this particular
New-England may be allowed to claim, I think, a
merit of a peculiar character. She early adopted
and has constantly maintained the principle, that
it is the undoubted right, and the bounden duty
of government, to provide for the instruction of all
youth. That which is elsewhere left to chance,
or to charity, we secure by law. For the purpose
of public instruction, we hold every man subject
to taxation in proportion to his property, and we
look not to the question, whether he himself
have, or have not; children to be benefited by the
education for which he pays. We regard it as a
wise and liberal system of police, by which property, and life, and the peace of society are secured. We seek to prevent, in some measure,
the extension of the penal code, by inspiring a
salutary and conservative principle of virtue and
of knowledge in an early age. We hope to excite a feeling of respectability, and a sense of character, by enlarging the capacity, and increasing
the sphere of intellectual enjoyment. By general

instruction, we seek, as far as possible, to purify the whole moral atmosphere ; to keep good sentiments uppermost, and to turn the strong current of feeling and opinion, as well as the censures of the law, and the denunciations of religion, against immorality and crime. We hope for a security, beyond the law, and above the law, in the prevalence of enlightened and well principled moral sentiment. We hope to continue and prolong the time, when, in the villages and farm houses of New-England, there may be undisturbed sleep within unbarred doors. And knowing that our government rests directly on the public will, that we may preserve it, we endeavour to give a safe and proper direction to that public will. We do not, indeed, expect all men to be philosophers or statesmen ; but we confidently trust, and our expectation of the duration of our system of government rests on that trust, that by the diffusion of general knowledge and good and virtuous sentiments, the political fabric may be secure, as well against open violence and overthrow, as against the slow but sure undermining of licentiousness.

12

We know, that at the present time, an attempt is making in the English Parliament to provide by law for the education of the poor, and that a gentleman of distinguished character, (Mr. Brougham) has taken the lead, in presenting a plan to government for carrying that purpose into effect. And yet, although the representatives of the three kingdoms listened to him with astonishment as well as delight, we hear no principles, with which we ourselves have not been familiar from youth ; we see nothing in the plan, but an approach towards that system which has been established in New-England for more than a century and a half. It is said that in England, not more than *one child in fifteen* possesses the means of being taught to read and write ; in Wales, *one in twenty ;* in France, until lately, when some improvement was made, not more than *one in thirty-five.* Now, it is hardly too strong to say, that in New-England, *every child possesses* such means. It would be difficult to find an instance to the contrary, unless where it should be owing to the negligence of the parent ;—and in truth the means are actually used and enjoyed by nearly every one.

A youth of fifteen, of either sex, who cannot both read and write, is very unfrequently to be found. Who can make this comparison, or contemplate this spectacle, without delight and a feeling of just pride? Does any history shew property more beneficently applied? Did any government ever subject the property of those who have estates, to a burden, for a purpose more favourable to the poor, or more useful to the whole community?

A conviction of the importance of public instruction was one of the earliest sentiments of our ancestors. No lawgiver of ancient or modern times has expressed more just opinions, or adopted wiser measures, than the early records of the Colony of Plymouth show to have prevailed here. Assembled on this very spot, a hundred and fifty-three years ago, the legislature of this Colony declared; " For as much as the maintenance of good literature doth much tend to the advancement of the weal and flourishing state of Societies and Republics, this Court doth therefore order, that in whatever township in this government, consisting of fifty families or upwards, any meet man shall be obtained to teach a grammar school, such township shall allow at least twelve pounds, to be raised by rate, on all the inhabitants."

Having provided, that all youth should be instructed in the elements of learning by the institution of Free Schools, our ancestors had yet another duty to perform. Men were to be educated for the professions, and the public. For this purpose they founded the University, and with incredible zeal and perseverance they cherished and supported it, through all trials and discouragements. On the subject of the University, it is not possible for a son of New-England to think without pleasure, nor to speak without emotion. Nothing confers more honour on the state where it is established, or more utility on the country at large. A respectable University is an establishment, which must be the work of time. If pecuniary means were not wanting, no new institution could possess character and respectability at once. We owe deep obligation to our ancestors, who began, almost on the moment of their arrival, the work of building up this institution.

Although established in a different government, the Colony of Plymouth manifested warm friendship for Harvard College. At an early period, its government took measures to promote a general subscription throughout all the towns in this Colony, in aid of its small funds. Other Colleges were subsequently founded and endowed, in other places, as the ability of the people allowed ; and we may flatter ourselves, that the means of education, at present enjoyed in New-England, are not only adequate to the diffusion of the elements of knowledge among all classes, but sufficient also for respectable attainments in literature and the sciences.

Lastly, our ancestors have founded their system of government on morality and religious sentiment. Moral habits, they believed, cannot safely be trusted on any other foundation than religious principle, nor any government be secure which is not supported by moral habits. Living under the heavenly light of revelation, they hoped to find all the social dispositions, all the duties which men owe˙ to each other and to society, enforced and performed. Whatever makes men good christians, makes them good citizens. Our fathers came here to enjoy their religion free and unmolested; and, at the end of two centuries, there is nothing upon which we can pronounce more confidently, nothing of which we can express a more deep and earnest conviction, than of the inestimable importance of that religion to man, both in regard to this life, and that which is to come.

If the blessings of our political and social condition have not now been too highly estimated, we cannot well over-rate the responsibility and duty which they impose upon us. We hold these institutions of government, religion, and learning, to be transmitted, as well as enjoyed. We are in the line of conveyance, through which whatever has been obtained by the spirit and efforts of our ancestors, is to be communicated to our children.

We are bound to maintain public liberty, and by the example of our own systems, to convince the world, that order, and law, religion and morality, the rights of conscience, the rights of persons, and the rights of property, may all be preserved and secured, in the most perfect manner, by a government entirely and purely elective. If we fail in this, our disaster will be signal, and will furnish an argument, stronger than has yet been found, in support of those opinions, which maintain that government can rest safely on nothing but power and coercion. As far as experience may show errors in our establishments, we are bound to correct them ; and if any practices exist, contrary to the principles of justice and humanity, within the reach of our laws or our influence, we are inexcusable if we do not exert ourselves to restrain and abolish them.

I deem it my duty on this occasion to suggest, that the land is not yet wholly free from the contamination of a traffic, at which every feeling of humanity must forever revolt—I mean the African slave trade. Neither public sentiment, nor the law, has hitherto been able entirely to put an end to this odious and abominable trade. At the moment when God, in his mercy, has blessed the Christian world with an universal peace, there is reason to fear, that to the disgrace of the Christian name and character, new efforts are making for the extension of this trade, by subjects and citizens of Christian states, in whose hearts no sentiment of humanity or justice inhabits, and over whom neither the fear of God nor the fear of man exercises a control. In the sight of our law, the African slave trader is a pirate and a felon; and in the sight of heaven, an offender far beyond the ordinary depth of human guilt. There is no brighter part of our history, than that which records the measures which have been adopted by the government, at an early day, and at different times since, for the suppression of this traffic; and I would call on all the true sons of New-England, to co-operate with the laws of man, and the justice of heaven. If there be, within the extent of our knowledge or influence, any participation in this traffic, let us pledge ourselves here, upon the Rock of Plymouth, to extirpate and destroy it. It is not fit, that the land of the Pilgrims should bear the shame longer. I hear the sound of the hammer, I see the smoke of the furnaces where manacles and fetters are still forged for human limbs. I see the visages of those, who by stealth, and at midnight, labour in this work of hell, foul and dark, as may become the artificers of such instruments of misery and torture. Let that spot be purified, or let it cease to be of New-England. Let it be purified, or let it be set aside from the Christian world; let it be put out of the circle of human sympathies and human regards, and let civilized man henceforth have no communion with it.

I would invoke those who fill the seats of justice, and all who minister at her altar, that they execute the wholesome and necessary severity of the law. I invoke the ministers of our religion, that they proclaim its denunciation of these crimes, and add its solemn sanctions to the authority of human laws. If the pulpit be silent, whenever, or wherever, there may be a sinner bloody with this guilt, within the hearing of its voice, the pulpit is false to its trust. I call on

13

the fair merchant, who has reaped his harvest upon the seas, that he assist in scourging from those seas the worst pirates which ever infested them. That ocean, which seems to wave with a gentle magnificence to waft the burdens of an honest commerce, and to roll along its treasures with a conscious pride ; that ocean, which hardy industry regards, even when the winds have ruffled its surface, as a field of grateful toil; what is it to the victim of this oppression, when he is brought to its shores, and looks forth upon it, for the first time, from beneath chains, and bleeding with stripes ? What is it to him, but a wide spread prospect of suffering, anguish and death? Nor do the skies smile longer, nor is the air longer fragrant to him. The sun is cast down from heaven. An inhuman and accursed traffic has cut him off in his manhood, or in his youth, from every enjoyment belonging to his being, and every blessing which his Creator intended for him.

The Christian communities send forth their emissaries of religion and letters, who stop, here and there, along the coast of the vast continent of Africa, and with painful and tedious efforts, make some almost imperceptible progress in 'the communication of knowledge, and in the general improvement of the natives who are immediately about them. Not thus slow and imperceptible is the transmission of the vices and bad passions which the subjects of Christian states carry to the land. The slave trade having touched the coast, its influence and its evils spread, like a pestilence, over the whole continent, making savage wars more savage, and more frequent, and adding new and fierce passions to the contests of barbarians.

I pursue this topic no further; except again to say, that all Christendom being now blessed with peace, is bound by every thing which belongs to its character, and to the character of the present age, to put a stop to this inhuman and disgraceful traffic.

We are bound not only to maintain the general principles of public liberty, but to support also those existing forms of government, which have so well secured its enjoyment, and so highly promoted the public prosperity. It is now more than thirty years that these States have been united under the Federal Constitution, and whatever fortune may await them hereafter, it is impossible that this period of their history should not be regarded as distinguished by signal prosperity and success. They must be sanguine, indeed, who can hope for benefit from change. Whatever division of the public judgment may have existed in relation to particular measures of the government, all must agree, one should think, in the opinion, that in its general course it has been eminently productive of public happiness. Its most ardent friends could not well have hoped from it more than it has accomplished ; and those who disbelieved or doubted ought to feel less concern about predictions, which the event has not verified, than pleasure in the good which has been obtained. Whoever shall hereafter write this part of our history, although he may see occasional errors or defects, will be able to record no great failure in the ends and objects of government. Still less will he be able to record any series of lawless and despotic acts, or any successful usurpation. His page will contain no exhibition of provinces depopulated, of civil authority habitually trampled down by military power, or of a community crushed by the burden of taxation. He will speak, rather, of public liberty protected, and public happiness advanced ; of increased revenue, and population augmented beyond all example ; of the growth of commerce, manufactures, and the arts ; and of that happy condition, in which the restraint and coercion of government are almost invisible and imperceptible, and its influence felt only in the benefits which it confers. We can entertain no better wish for our country than that this government may be preserved ; nor have we a clearer duty than to maintain and support it in the full exercise of all its just constitutional powers.

The cause of science and literature also imposes upon us an important and delicate trust. The wealth and population of the country are now so far advanced, as to authorize the expectation of a correct literature, and a well formed taste, as well as respectable progress in the abstruse sciences. The country has risen from a state of colonial dependency ; it has established an independent government, and is now in the undisturbed enjoyment of peace and political security. The elements of knowledge are universally diffused, and the reading portion of the community large. Let us hope that the present may be an auspicious era of literature. If, almost on the day of their landing, our ancestors founded schools and endowed colleges, what obligations do not rest upon us, living under circumstances so much more favourable both for providing and for using the means of education ? Literature becomes free institutions. It is the graceful ornament of civil liberty, and a happy restraint on the asperities, which political controversy sometimes occasions. Just taste is not only an embellishment of society, but it rises almost to the rank of the virtues, and diffuses positive good throughout the whole extent of its influence. There is a connexion between right feeling and right principles, and truth in taste is allied with truth in morality. With nothing in our past history to discourage us, and with something in our present condition and prospects to animate us, let us hope, that as it is our fortune to live in an age when we may behold a wonderful advancement of the country in all its other great interests, we may see also equal progress and success attend the cause of letters.

Finally, let us not forget the religious character of our origin. Our fathers were brought hither by their high veneration for the Christian Religion. They journeyed by its light, and laboured in its hope. They sought to incorporate its principles with the elements of their society, and to diffuse its influence through all their institutions, civil, political, or literary. Let us cherish these sentiments, and extend this influence still more widely ; in the full conviction, that that is the happiest society, which partakes in the highest degree of the mild and peaceable spirit of Christianity.

The hours of this day are rapidly flying, and this occasion will soon be passed. Neither we nor our children can expect to behold its return. They are in the distant regions of futurity, they exist only in the all-creating power of God, who shall stand here, a hundred years hence, to trace, through us, their descent from the Pilgrims, and to survey, as we have now surveyed, the progress of their country, during the lapse of a century. We would anticipate their concurrence with us in our sentiments of deep regard for our common ancestors. We would anticipate and partake the pleasure with which they will then recount the steps of New-England's advancement. On the morning of that day, although it will not disturb us in our repose, the voice of acclamation and gratitude, commencing on the Rock of Plymouth, shall be transmitted through millions of the sons of the Pilgrims, till it lose itself in the murmurs of the Pacific seas.

We would leave for the consideration of those who shall then occupy our places, some proof that we hold the blessings transmitted from our fathers in just estimation ; some proof of our attachment to the cause of good government,

and of civil and religious liberty ; some proof
of a sincere and ardent desire to promote every
thing which may enlarge the understandings and
improve the hearts of men. And when, from
the long distance of an hundred years, they shall
look back upon us, they shall know, at least,
that we possessed affections, which running backward, and warming with gratitude for what our
ancestors have done for our happiness, run forward also to our posterity, and meet them with
cordial salutation, ere yet they have arrived on
the shore of Being.

Advance, then, ye future generations ! We
would hail you, as you rise in your long succession, to fill the places which we now fill, and to
taste the blessings of existence, where we are
passing, and soon shall have passed, our own human duration. We bid you welcome to this
pleasant land of the Fathers. We bid you welcome to the healthful skies, and the verdant
fields of New-England. We greet your accession to the great inheritance which we have enjoyed. We welcome you to the blessings of

good government, and religious liberty. We welcome you to the treasures of science, and the delights of learning. We welcome you to the transcendant sweets of domestic life, to the happiness of kindred, and parents, and children. We welcome you to the immeasurable blessings of rational existence, the immortal hope of Christianity, and the light of everlasting Truth!

Appendix.

The following is a list of the DISCOURSES delivered on this Anniversary. Those marked with an asterisk have not been printed.

1769. First publicly noticed by the *Old Colony Club.*
1770. EDWARD WINSLOW, jun. Esq. of *Plymouth*, an Oration.*
1771. (Lord's Day) the next day (23d) a public dinner.
1772. Rev. CHANDLER ROBBINS, of *Plymouth*, on Ps. lxxviii. 6. 7.*
1773. Rev. CHARLES TURNER, *Duxbury*, Zeck. iv. 10.
1774. Rev. GAD HITCHCOCK, *Pembroke*, Gen. i. 31.
1775. Rev. SAMUEL BALDWIN, *Hanover*, Heb. xi. 8.
1776. Rev. SYLVANUS CONANT, *Middleborough*, Exod. i. 12.
1777. Rev. SAMUEL WEST, *Dartmouth*, Isai. lxvi. 5—9.
1778. Rev. TIMOTHY HILLIARD, *Barnstable.**
1779. Rev. WILLIAM SHAW, *Marshfield.**
1780. Rev. JONATHAN MOORE, *Rochester*, Isai. xli. 10. 11.*
       From this time the public observance of the day was suspended, till
1794. Rev. CHANDLER ROBBINS, D.D. *Plymouth*, Psal. lxxvii. 11.
1795. ⎫
1796. ⎬ Private celebration.
1797. ⎭
1798. Doct. ZACHEUS BARTLETT, *Plymouth*, an Oration.*
1799. The day was so near that appointed for the ordination of the
       Rev. Mr. KENDALL, that it was not celebrated by a public dis-
       course.
1800. JOHN DAVIS, Esq. *Boston*, an Oration.*
1801. Rev. JOHN ALLYN, *Duxbury*, Heb. xii. 2.
1802. JOHN QUINCY ADAMS, Esq., *Boston*, an Oration.
1803. Rev. JOHN T. KIRKLAND, D.D. *Boston*, Prov. xvii. 6.*
1804. (Lord's Day) Rev. JAMES KENDALL, of *Plymouth*, preached from
       Heb. xi. 13.*
1805. ALDEN BRADFORD, Esq. *Wiscasset*, Exod. xii. 14.
1806. Rev. ABIEL HOLMES, D.D. *Cambridge*, Romans. xi. 5.

1807. Rev. JAMES FREEMAN, *Boston.**
1808. Rev. THADDEUS M. HARRIS, *Dorchester,* Ps. xliv. 1. 2. 3.
1809. Rev. ABIEL ABBOTT, *Beverly,* Deut. xxxii. 11. 12.
1810. Private celebration.
1811. (Lord's Day) Rev. JOHN ELIOT, D.D. *Boston.**
1812.
1813. } Private celebration.
1814.
1815. Rev. JAMES FLINT, *Bridgewater,* Ps. xvi. 6.
1816. (Lord's Day) Rev. EZRA GOODWIN, *Sandwich,* Isai. ix. 22.
1817. Rev. HORACE HOLLEY, *Boston.**
1818. WENDELL DAVIS, Esq. *Sandwich,* an Oration.*
1819. FRANCIS C. GRAY, Esq. *Boston,* an Oration.*
1820. Hon. DANIEL WEBSTER, *Boston,* an Oration.

ImTheStory.com

Personalized Classic Books in many genre's

Unique gift for kids, partners, friends, colleagues

Customize:

- Character Names
- Upload your own front/back cover images (optional)
- Inscribe a personal message/dedication on the
  inside page (optional)

Customize many titles Including
- Alice in Wonderland
- Romeo and Juliet
- The Wizard of Oz
- A Christmas Carol
- Dracula
- Dr. Jekyll & Mr. Hyde
- And more...

CPSIA information can be obtained at www.ICGtesting.com
Printed in the USA
LVOW01s0226120215

426721LV00031B/688/P